I0494570

GIFTED:
Art Quilts featuring
African American History Makers

by

Aisha Lumumba

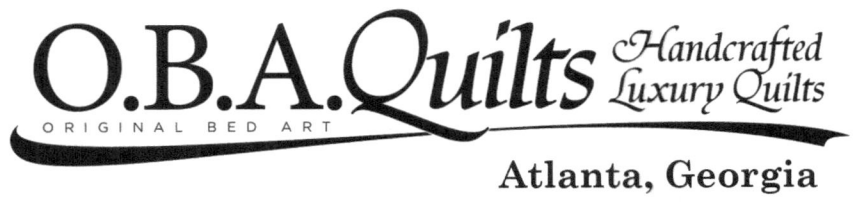

Atlanta, Georgia

© 2012 Aisha Lumumba
All rights reserved

No part of this publication may be reproduced, stored in a retrieval system, or transmitted in any form or by any means, electronic, mechanical, photocopying, recording or otherwise, without prior written permission from the author.

ISBN 13: 978-0-9639594-8-5
ISBN 10: 0-9639594-8-4

Photography: Jabari Lumumba and Aisha Lumumba
Cover Design: Aisha Lumumba

Acknowledgement

"The function of art is to do more than tell it like it is: It's to imagine what is possible."
~bell hooks

This series of art quilts could not have happened without the unending support and help of my spouse, Chinyelu Lumumba. I am forever grateful for his patience. The support of my entire family (immediate and extended) is so overwhelmingly wonderful that I could not name them all here but would like to say that they are all included in my gratitude.

I'd like to thank Jabari Lumumba for his great photography. Extreme gratitude goes to Sharifa Lumumba and Jamal Pope for the expert graphic support and advice. Thanks to J. Stacey Grayson, Cynthia P. Laster, Clara P. Wright, Mary E. Sirmans Johnson, and Sharifa Lumumba for keeping my words on the right path.

Many thanks to Malaika and Anane Lumumba for the greatest marketing ideas and help ever.

Appreciation and much gratitude to Kyra Hicks for writing **How To Self-Publish Your Own Quilt Catalog**. Her book is the reason this book was born.

I have some really good friends who are always there even when they are away doing other things. Thank you Elaine Parker, Pamela Diana, Brenda LeGrier and Marquetta Johnson. I'd also like to give an extra thanks to Marquetta Johnson for all the delightful hand-dyed fabric used in my quilts.

Thanks and love to all of the people that encouraged me to develop this quilting technique. Special thanks to the National Black Arts Festival and the Birmingham Public Library for being among the first to feature this exhibit.

Introduction

Africans have explored the use of fiber in art for centuries; however, the modern techniques developed here in America over the last two or more decades have slowly begun to revolutionize the process. Quilt-making purely for artistic value is relatively new to the genre of quilting. Great artists such as Faith Ringgold and Romare Bearden have set the standards high. But the newness of utilizing fabric as an art medium has not hindered my ability nor my zeal to jump right in and experiment with new ideas, designs and processes.

The History Makers series was first inspired by African American winners of the coveted Academy award, better known as The Oscar. Having no idea that the number of Black recipients was so low (with even fewer African American women), my interest was piqued into examining the award process even more. Several African Americans have been added to the list since I first started the series, so there is some catching up to do.

The Oprah Winfrey quilt was an idea that had been turning in my head for some time, even before Janelle Dowell announced the call for artists to help her create a visual tribute to Ms. Winfrey. It was my idea to give a glimpse of a private moment between best friends, such as a whisper of a joke "for your ears only". Many of my original sketches were rejected by my close critics because Oprah and Gayle were standing too close together (It seems that even at this point in history, any close friendship between women is subject to undue scrutiny.) As you can tell from the final version they were moved further apart but the big smile on Oprah's face tells the tale of the moment.

The election of Barack Obama as the 44th President of the United States was a milestone event never before witnessed in my lifetime until now. After wishing a thousand times that my father could have seen it, the enjoyment seeped in. It filled Black Americans with pride. The old adage, "you can be whatever you want to be," finally came true. The message behind the image is that the Obamas have stepped onto the dance floor of politics with elegance, grace and style. Michelle Obama's dress is red for a reason. It depicts the fire and strength that she has constantly shown. She is a great woman standing next to a great man.

The Josephine Baker quilt graced the annual gala of Alliance Française d'Atlanta . Of course the quilt was inspired by her reputation of dance and exquisite costumes.

The Michael Jackson quilt embodies the idea of the magic of Michael's genius. It was part of a butterfly themed exhibit I did, shortly after his death. This quilt would be the first of my many quilt tributes to his greatness.

The Rosa Parks quilt stirred quite a bit of controversy among my private critics because in her later years she wore glasses. Creating a young Rosa without glasses was just the statement as an artist that I wanted to make.

The Harriet Tubman quilt was a commissioned piece for Ms. Woodie Persons of Atlanta, Georgia. One of my favorite quotes of all time is from Harriet Tubman, "I freed a thousand slaves. I could have freed a thousand more if only they knew they were slaves." It is bordered with the quilt blocks now known to be a part of the Underground Railroad Quilt Code.

It is with sincere delight that I bring this series of art quilts to you in book form. Hopefully, it makes my great pleasure, your pleasure as well!

List

1. Elegance -a portrait quilt of President and Mrs. Barak Obama. President Obama is the 44th President of the United States and the first African American to hold the office.
2. First In Line -a portrait of Ms. Hattie McDaniel who was the first African American to win an Academy Award for her role as Mammy in the 1938 "Gone With Wind" movie.
3. Mr. Magic -a portrait quilt of Micheal Jackson, known as the King of Pop. He was an African American recording artist, entertainer and businessman. Jackson's 1982 album "Thriller" is the best-selling album of all time.
4. My Own Terms -a portrait quilt of Ms. Whoopi Goldberg, the African American comedian and actress that won her second Golden Globe and the Academy Award for the role of Oda Mae in the blockbuster film "Ghost".
5. My Reflection -a portrait quilt of Ray Charles and Jamie Foxx. The larger face is Ray Charles with Jamie Foxx reflected in the glasses. Jamie Foxx won an Academy Award for his performance as Ray Charles in the 2006 film "Ray".
6. Stunning - a portrait quilt of Ms. Josephine Baker. She was an African American dancer, singer and actress who found fame in France. Baker was the first African American to star in a major motion picture, first to integrate an American concert hall, and first to become a world-famous entertainer. She is also noted for her contributions to the Civil Rights Movement in the United States.
7. Urban Daze -a portrait quilt of Denzel Washington. He is the second African American male (after Sidney Poitier) to win the Academy Award for his role in the 2001 film "Training Day."
8. Lady Sings -a portrait quilt of Billie Holiday (Eleanora Fagan), an African American jazz singer and songwriter. She was nicknamed "Lady Day" by her friend and musical partner Lester Young.
9. Make Peace with Your Shadow -a portrait quilt of Morgan Freeman, an African American actor, film director, aviator, and narrator. He won the Academy Award in 2005 for "Million Dollar Baby." He has also won a Golden Globe and a Screen Actors Guild Award (SAG).

List

10. Taking a Stand -a portrait quilt of Ms. Rosa Parks, known as "the first lady of civil rights." In 1955, Ms. Parks refused to obey the bus driver that ordered her to give up her seat for a white passenger.

11. Rock My Soul -This quilt celebrates the great skills of African American Musicians honored with the Academy Award. From left to right-top to bottom:Isaac Hayes, Herbie Hancock, Irene Cara, Russell Williams II, Lionel Richie, Willie D. Burton, Prince, Quincy Jones, Stevie Wonder, and Three Six Mafia (Jordon Houston, Cedric Coleman, & Paul Beauregard).

12. No Trees Just Forest -a traditional patterned quilt with pictures of Forest Whitaker. He is an actor, producer, and director. Mr. Whitaker won an Academy Award for his performance as Ugandan dictator Idi Amin in the 2006 film "The Last King of Scotland."

13. Leading Lady -a portrait quilt of Ms. Halle Berry, an African American actress and former fashion model. Ms. Berry received an Emmy, Golden Globe, Screen Actors Guild Award (SAG), and a NAACP Image Award for "Introducing Dorothy Dandridge" and won an Academy Award for Best Actress in her 2001 performance in "Monster's Ball."

14. They Call Me Mister -a portrait quilt of Sidney Poitier. In 1963, Mr. Poitier became the first black person to win an Academy Award for Best Actor for his role in "Lilies of the Field."

15. BFF - a portrait quilt of Ms. Oprah Winfrey and Ms. Gayle King. It is a depiction of their close friendship. Ms. Winfrey and Ms. King have become well known for their work in the mass media.

16 Nothing Like Coming Home -this quilt is homage to Julie Dash, for her 1991 independent film, "Daughters of the Dust" which tells the story of three generations of Gullah women at the turn of the 20th century.

17. Biggie -a portrait quilt of Biggie Smalls (Christopher Wallace), a very popular rapper, who is notably known as Notorious B.I.G.

18. Ms. Harriet -a portrait quilt of Harriet Tubman. After escaping from slavery, into which she was born, she made missions to rescue many more.

19. The Fiddler -a portrait quilt of Louis Gossett, Jr. The quilt was name the fiddler after his Emmy Award winning role in the television mini-series "Roots." He also won an Academy Award for his role as Gunnery Sergeant Emil Foley in the 1982 film "An Officer and A Gentleman."

Aisha Lumumba

I was born in Georgia in a rural suburb of Atlanta, known as McDonough, in the mid 1950's. I now live in Atlanta, and have a passion for many artistic mediums. My interest in art started at a very early age. I learned quilting by watching the elders make utilitarian quilts. My first love was sewing and creating art projects with fabric which eventually led me to quilting. I started my first quilt at age 18 and now I have more than 25 years of quilting experience, not only practical uses, but as a form of artistic expression.

I was a high achiever as I matriculated through the Henry County school system. After moving to Atlanta, I attended Georgia State University, only to become a mediocre art major. I started a family with my husband, Chinyelu Lumumba while still attending Georgia State University. He introduced me to books by and about black people that I never knew existed. With zeal and excitement I read every book I could get my hands on about black history. During this period of awakening, I changed my name from my birth name to Aisha. This awareness of the "black struggle" and black people's contribution to life (in Africa, America and throughout the world) added new meaning to my life and expression to my artistic desires.

As a young child I saw very few positive images of myself and others that looked like me in media (print or visual). When I attended Georgia State where we were asked to draw pictures off the top of our heads, I couldn't come up with anything. Now I realize that images did in fact come to me but I rejected them because I subconsciously thought they were not acceptable images. I had not seen art depicting two barefooted black girls running down a dusty dirt road, or pears lined up in buckets on my grandmother's back porch, or the decaying homes of our neighborhood. So I convinced myself that I was not a good artist because I couldn't visualize a sliced apple on a pristine dining plate. As the years went by, the thought occurred to me that I had a right to create art that featured the images of my reality. Of course things had changed drastically in the world and I was seeing pictures of us, but more often than not they were degrading pictures. I set out to create self-affirming positive images of ourselves and our lives through my art.

So there you have it. I am an African American artist that unashamedly creates African American art. What a novel idea! I appeared on TV One's Living With Soul, WSB's People to People twice, and interviewed by various other media affiliates. I published two cookbooks, a novel and was featured in **A Time, A Season: A Visual Tribute to Oprah Winfrey spearheaded** by Janelle Dowell, **I Now Have A Ribbon** by Ken Gehle, and **Artistic Expressions by Quilters of Color** by Ebony Stitchers Quilt Guild. I installed Quilt Exhibits in many places, namely five (5) consecutive years at The Atrium on Auburn Art Gallery Atlanta, Georgia; Birmingham Public Library Art Gallery Birmingham, Alabama; and the National Black Arts Festival Atlanta, Georgia. I have also exhibited in many quilt and art shows throughout the country: California, Alabama, Florida, North Carolina, and of course Georgia.

Now I am a very prolific, full-time artist possessing memberships in Brown Sugar Stitchers Quilt Guild, Black Art in America Art Group, and African Americans for the Arts. My quilts are now a part of the private collections of many individual collections, including those of Ambassador Andrew Young, Mrs. Valerie Jackson, Dr. Stephanie Jolly, Ms. Brenda Banks, Ms. Woodie Persons, Jualynne E. Dodson, and President & Mrs. Barack Obama, as well as displayed in The Atrium on Sweet Auburn in the Oddfellows Historic Building located in Atlanta, Georgia.

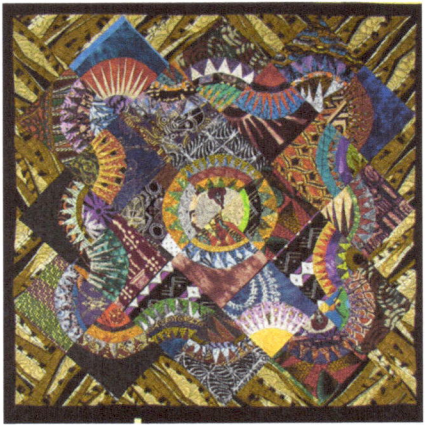

**The Stars Come Out
2007**

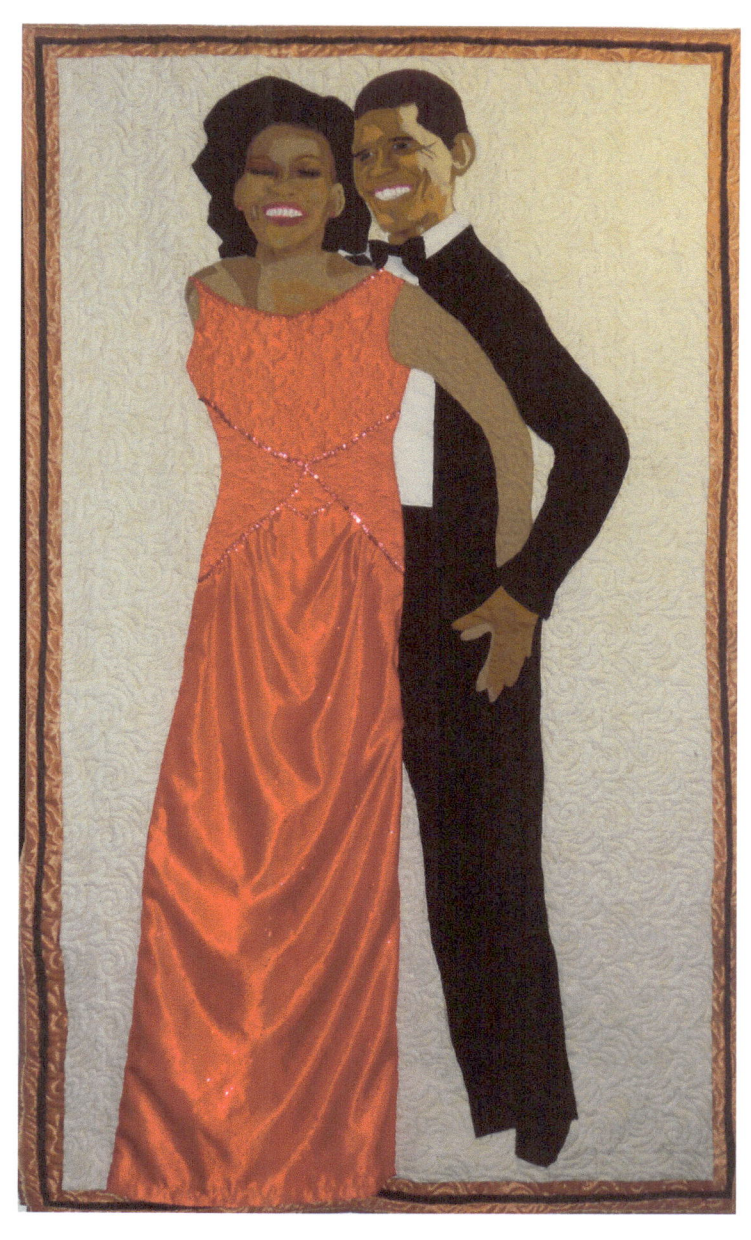

"Elegance"
President Barak Obama and First Lady Michelle Obama
46"x76"
2011

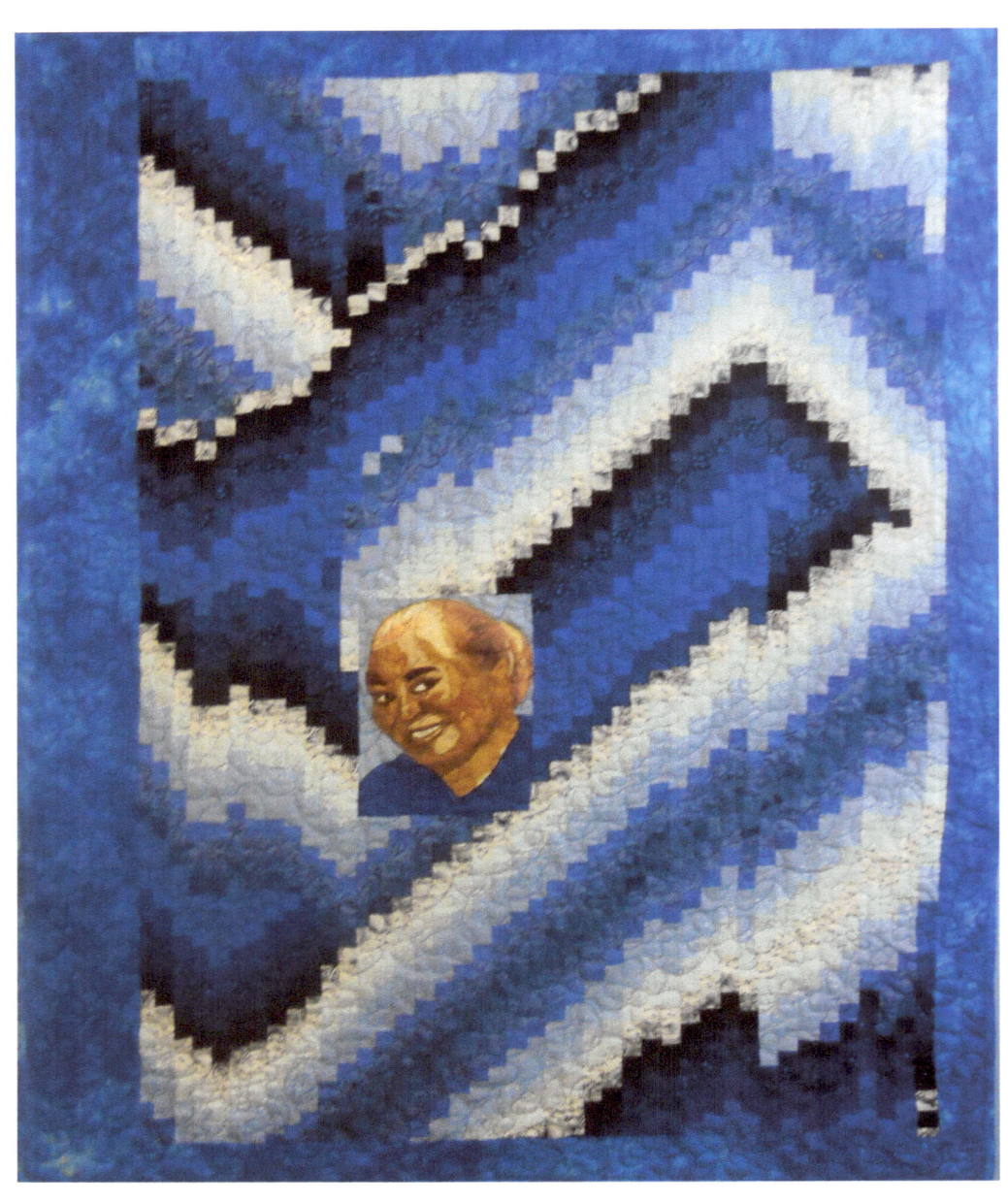

"First in Line"
Hattie McDaniel
44"x54"
2009

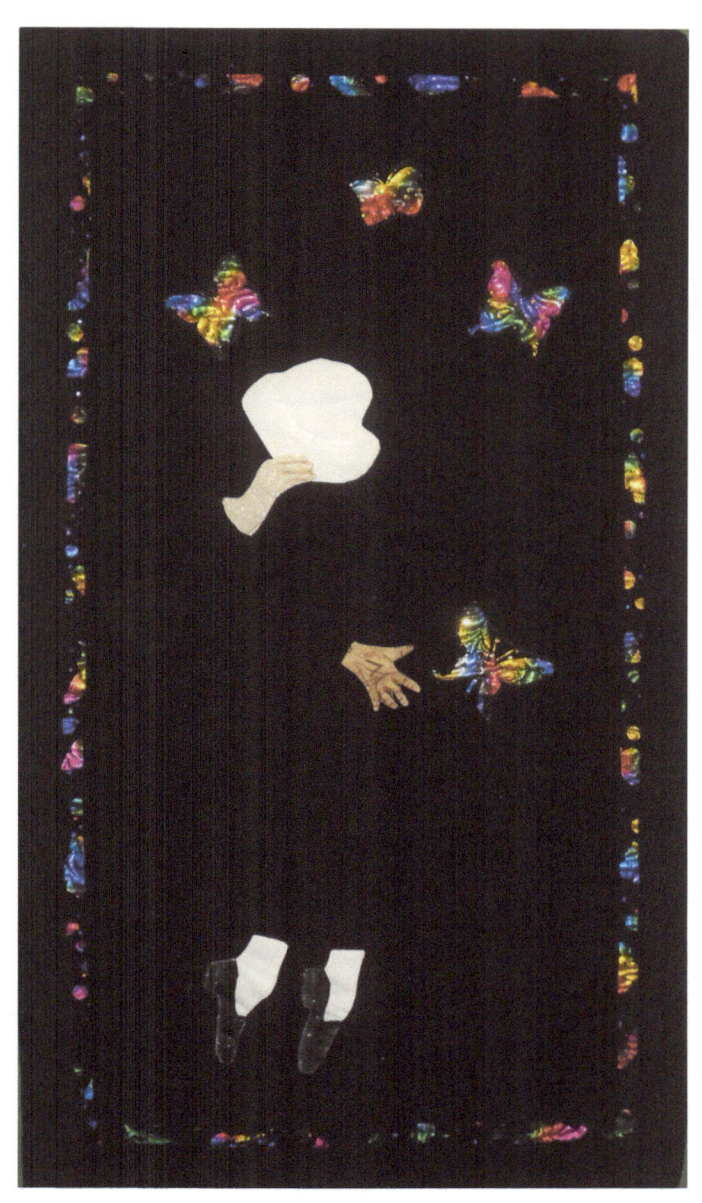

"Mr. Magic"
Michael Jackson
33"x53"
2010

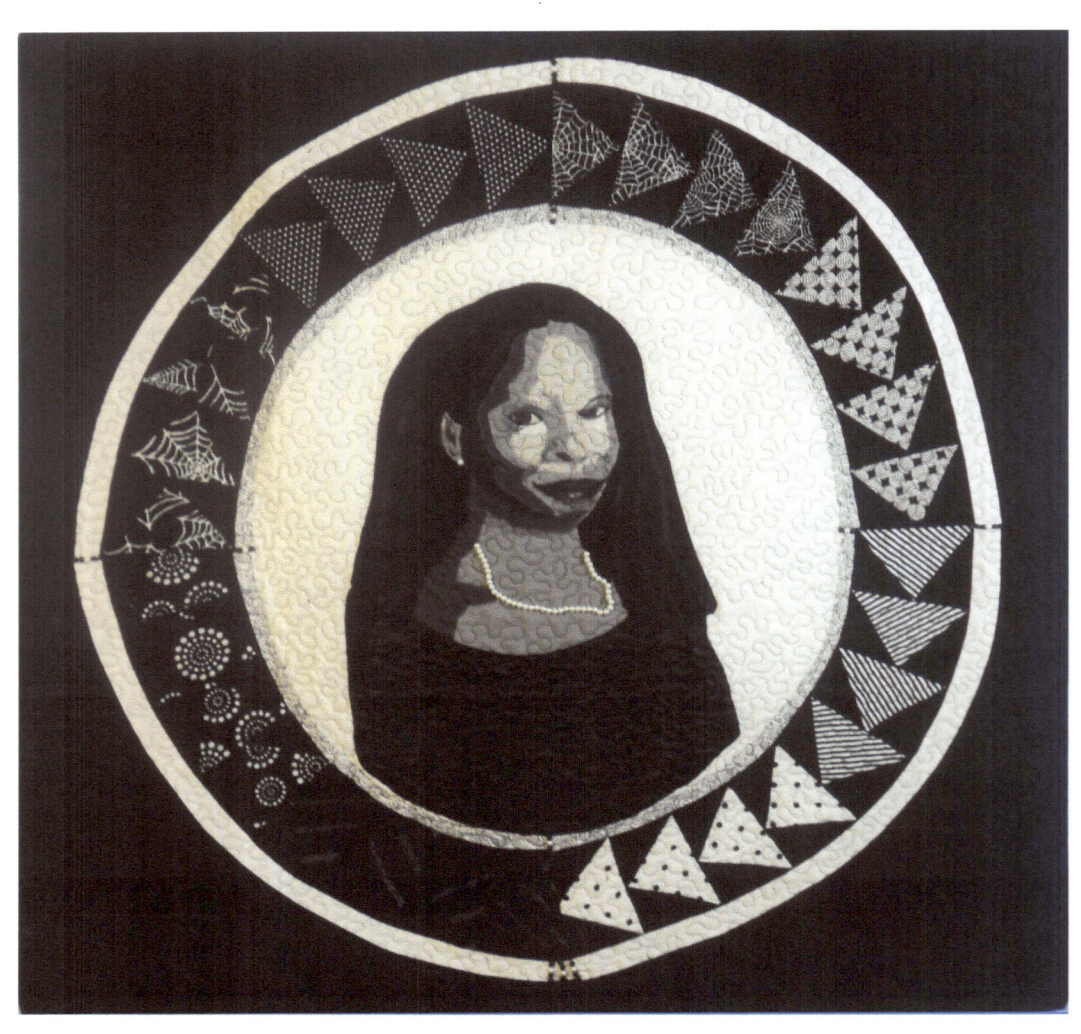

"My Own Terms"
Whoopi Goldberg
42"x41"
2009

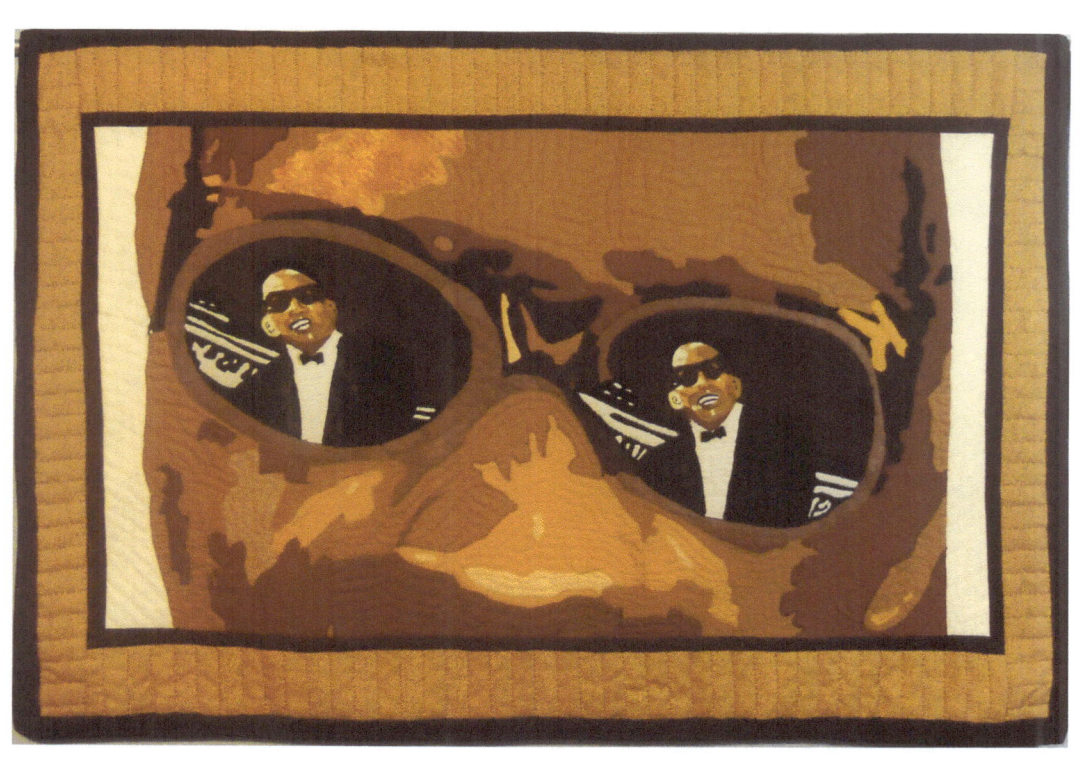

"My Reflection"
Jamie Foxx
52"x36"
2009

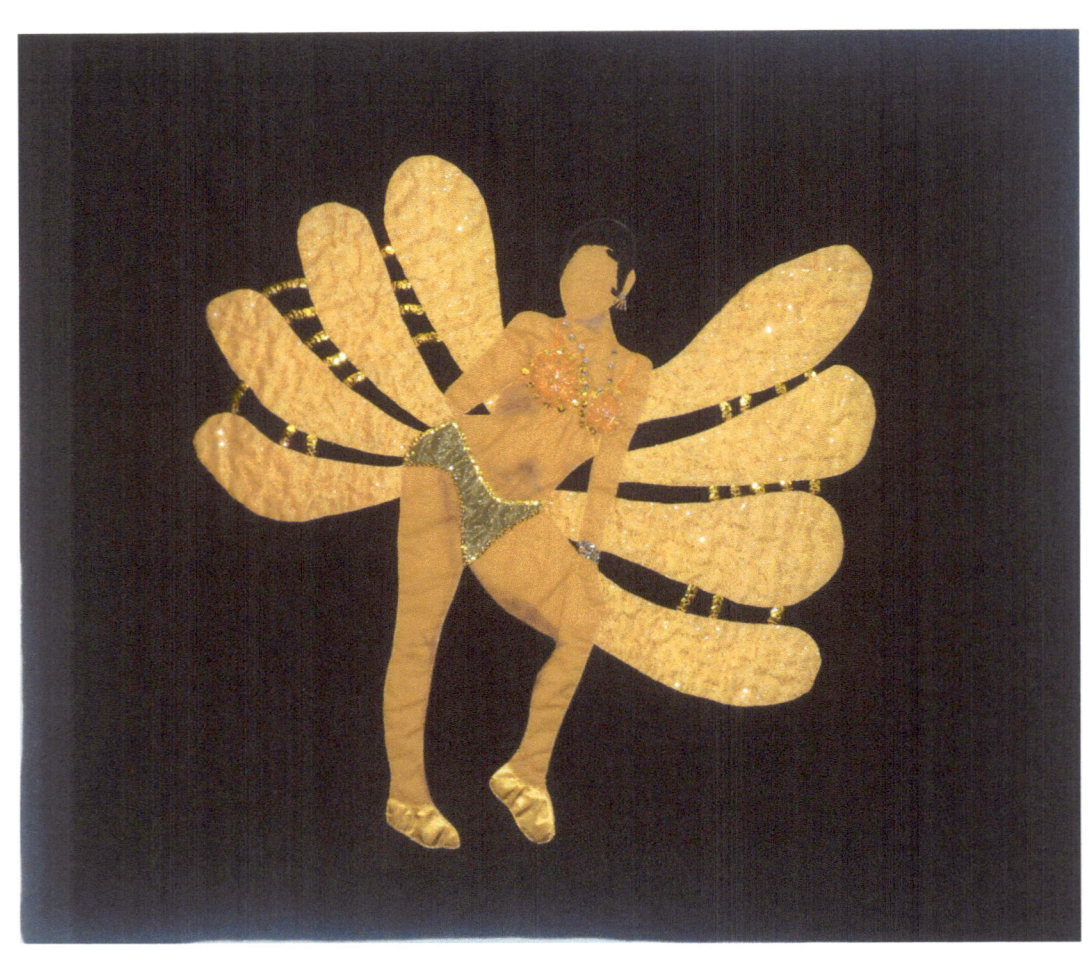

"Stunning"
Josephine Baker
43"x38"
2009

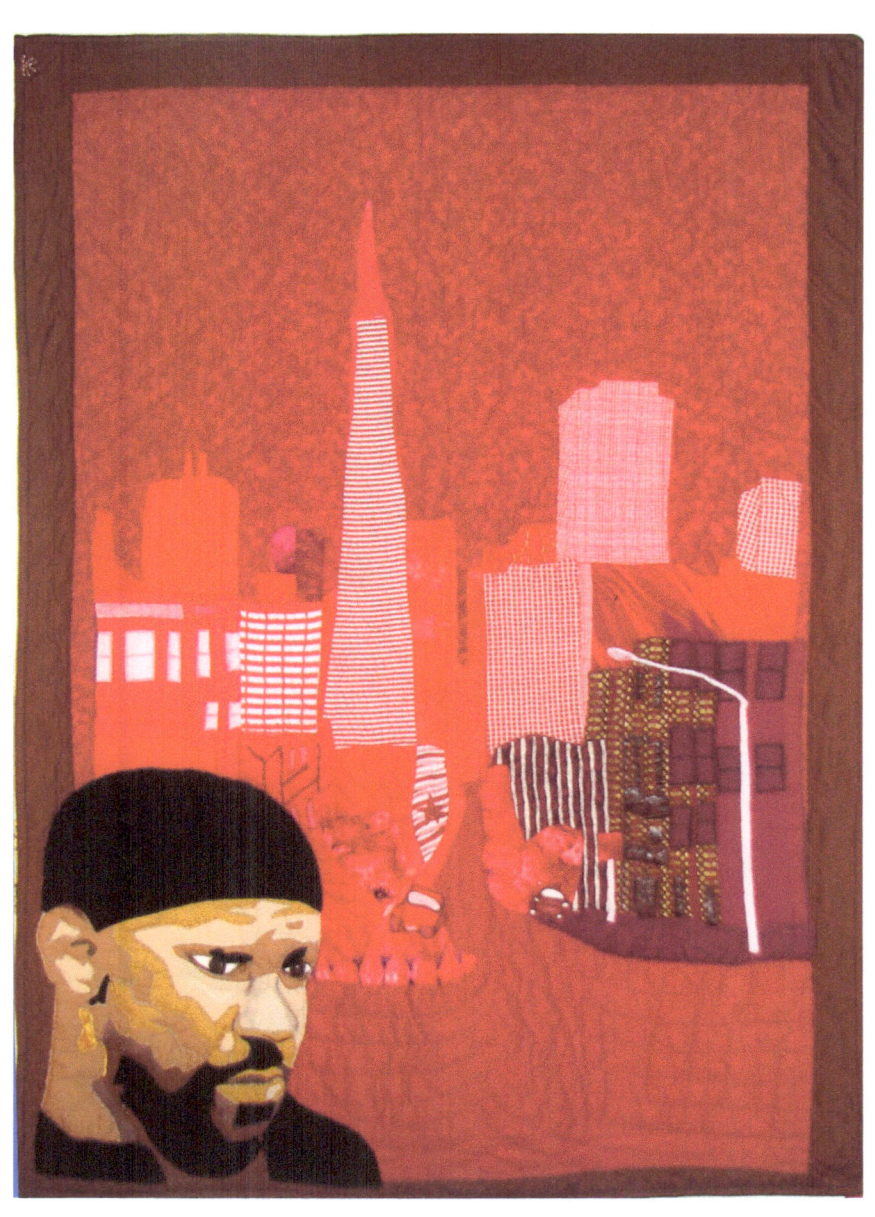

"Urban Daze"
Denzel Washington
39"x53"
2009

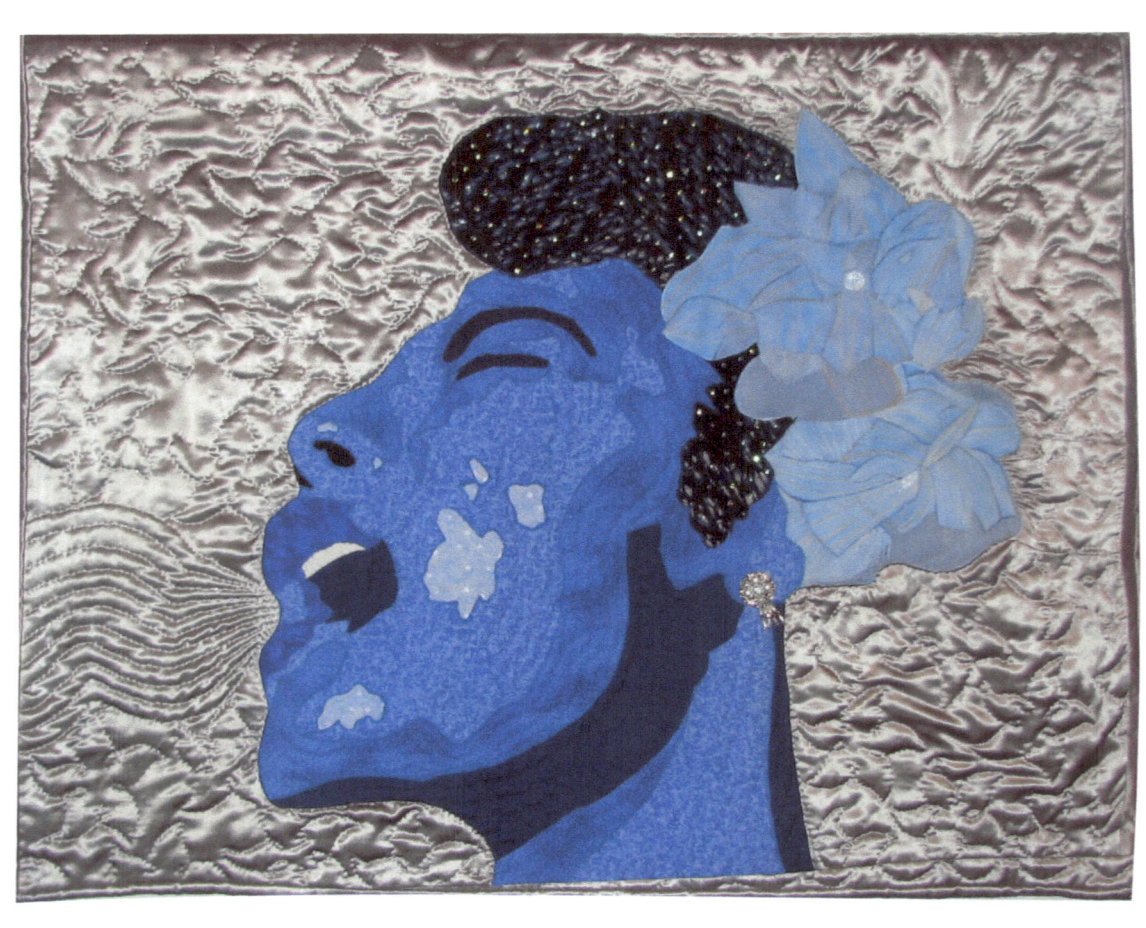

"Lady Sings"
Billie Holiday
48"x39"
2010

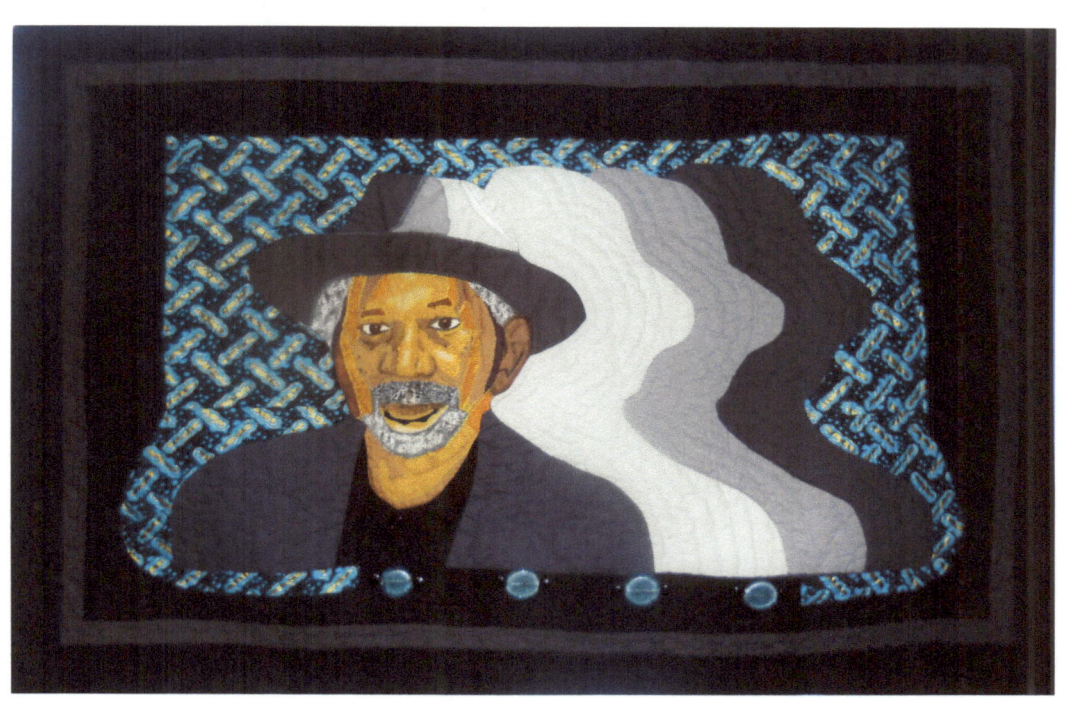

"Make Peace With Your Shadow"
Morgan Freeman
43"x29"
2009

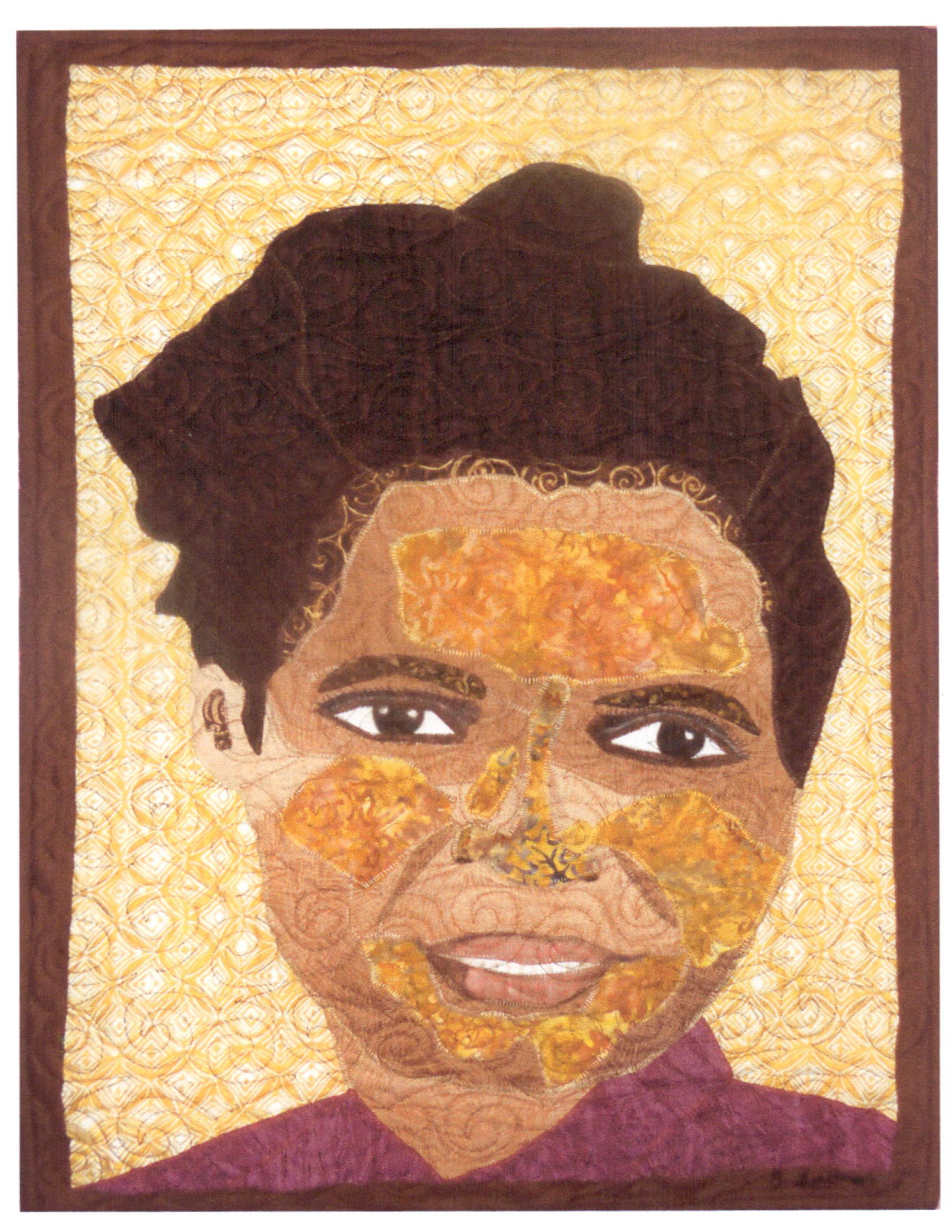

"Taking A Stand"
Rosa Parks
33"x35"
2011

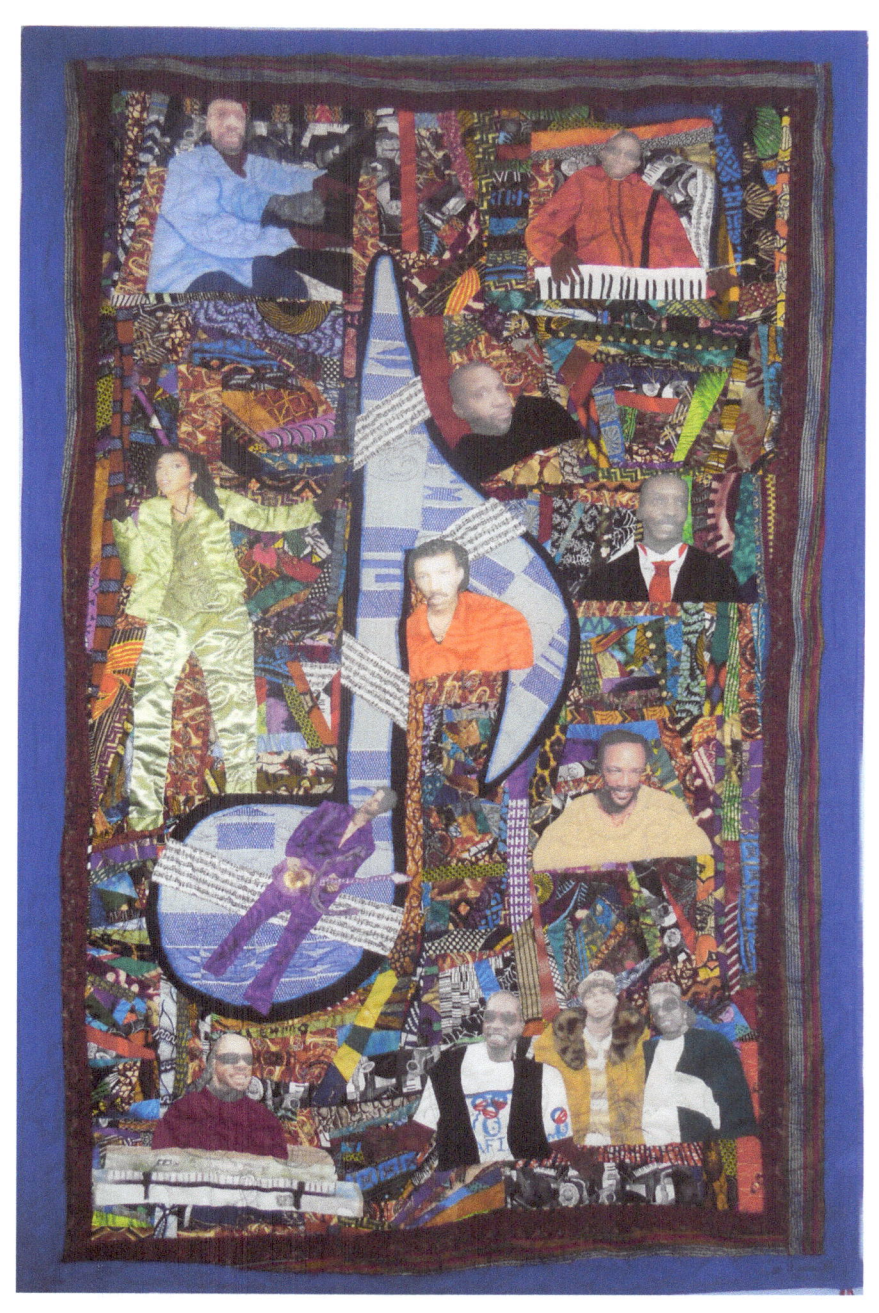

"Rock My Soul"
Musicians
50"x77"
2009

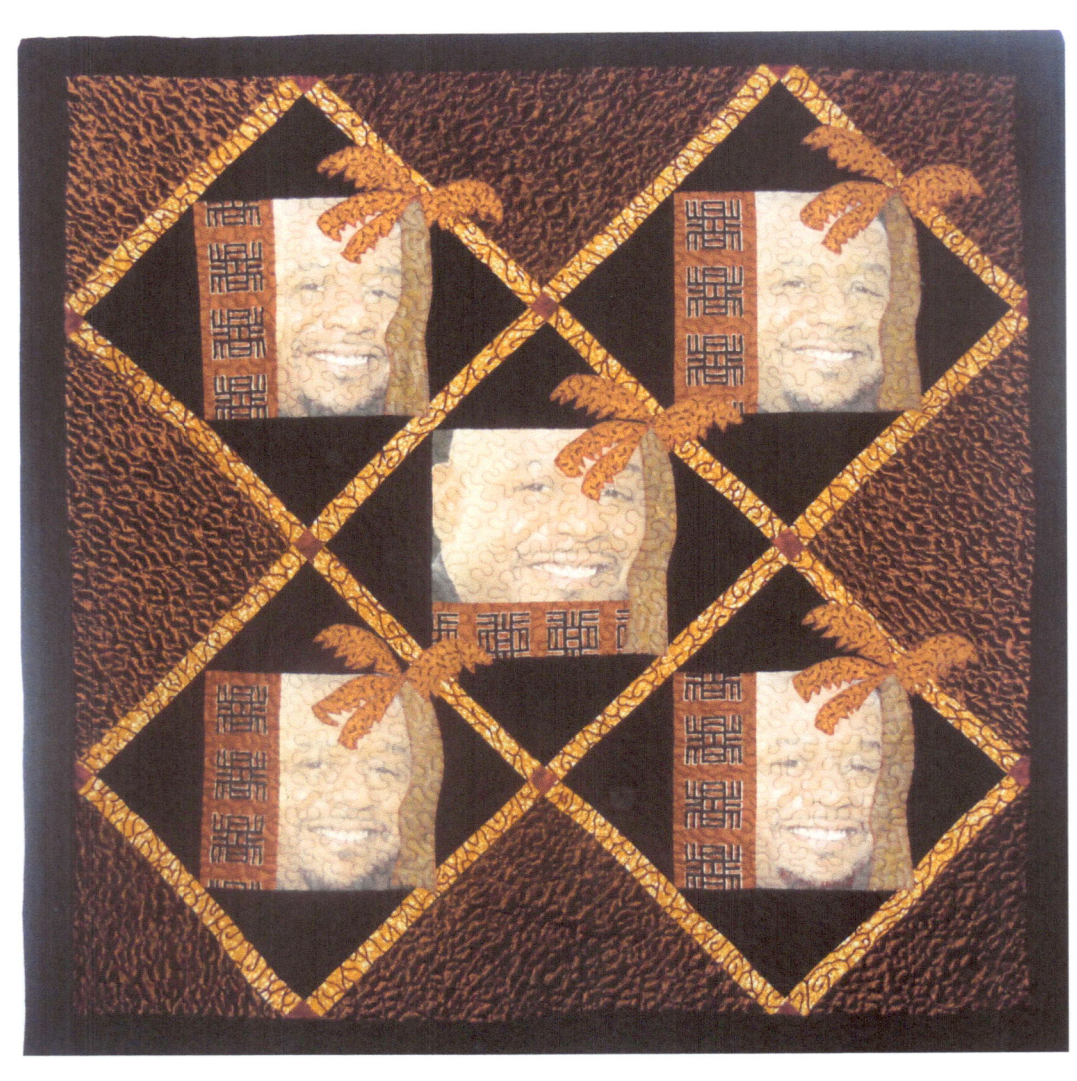

"No Trees Just Forest"
Forest Whitaker
46"x47"
2009

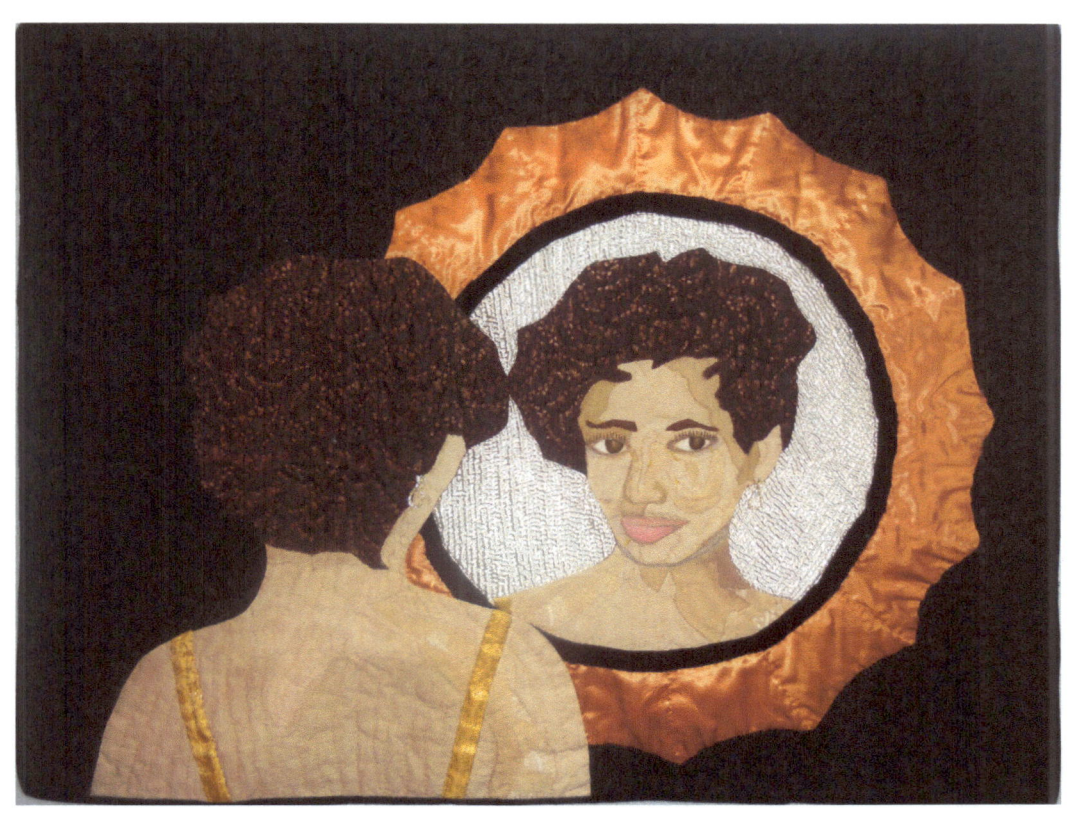

"Leading Lady"
Halle Berry
50"x38"
2009

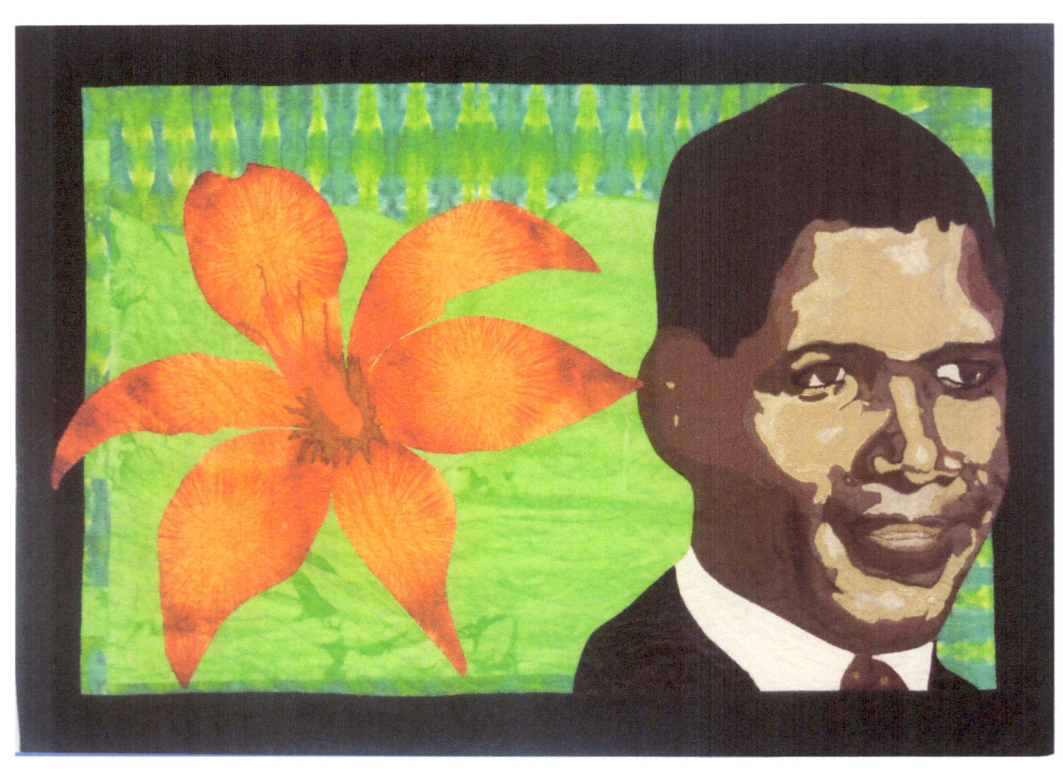

"They Call Me Mister"
Sidney Poitier
56"x40"
2009

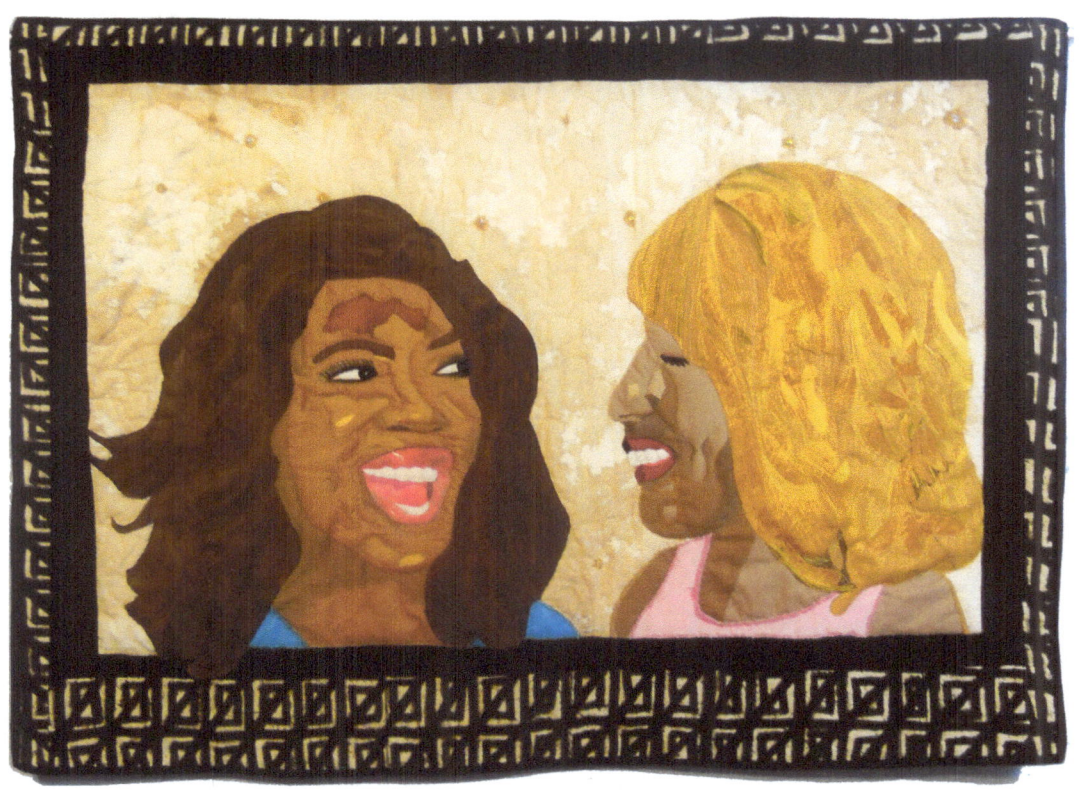

"BFF"
Oprah Winfrey and Gayle King
50"x38"
2010

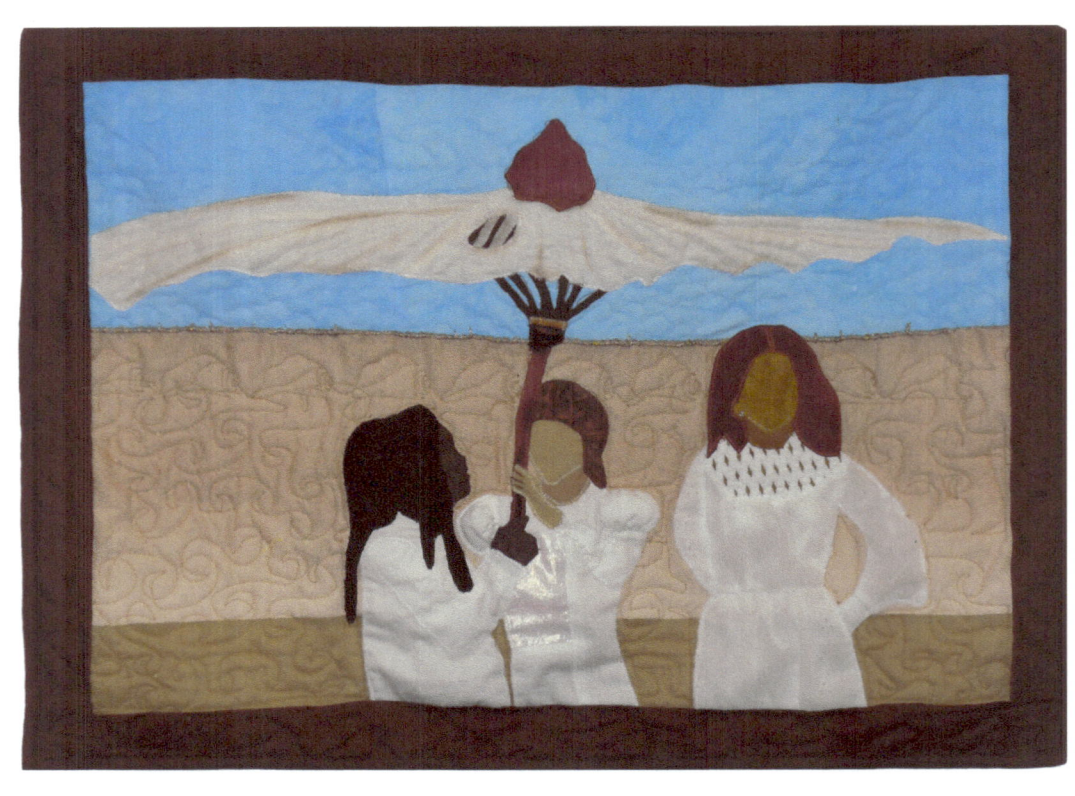

"Nothing Like Coming Home"
Tribute to Julie Dash
24.5"x33"
2011

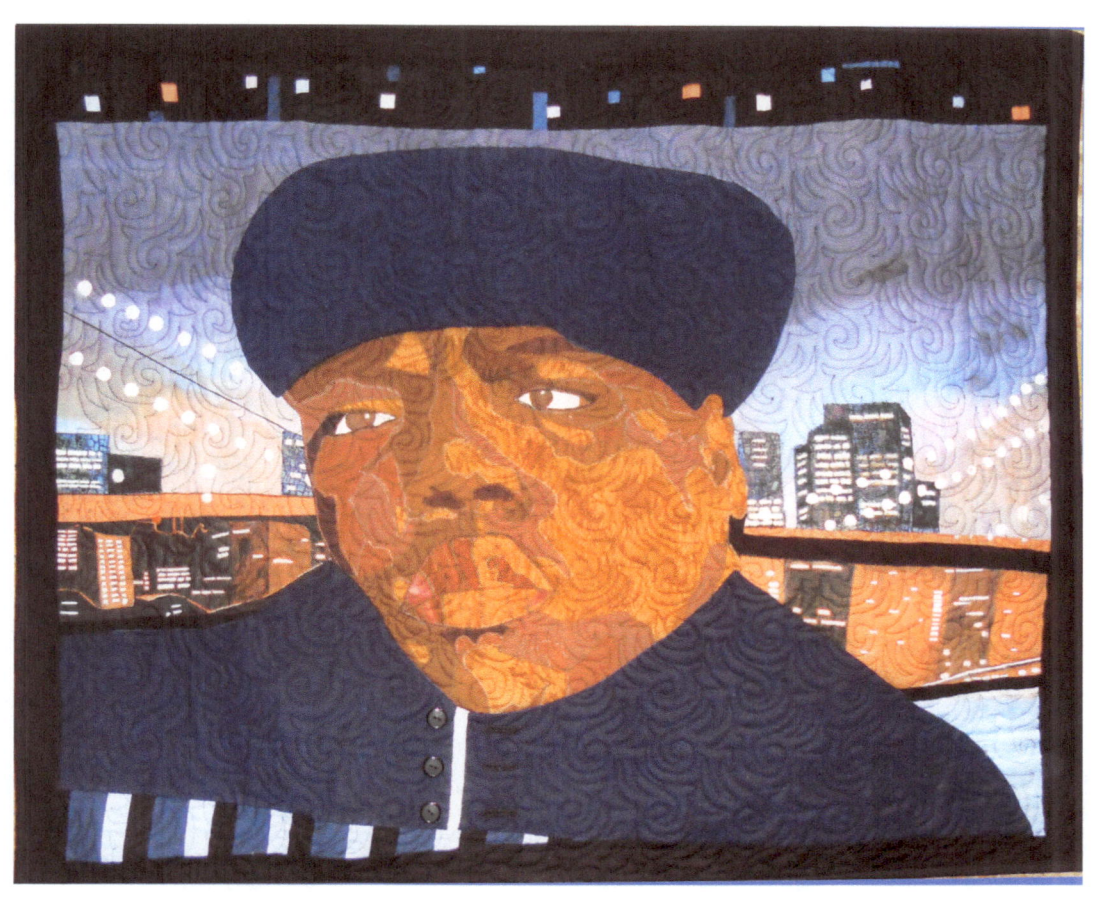

"Biggie"
Biggie Smalls
45"x42"
2011

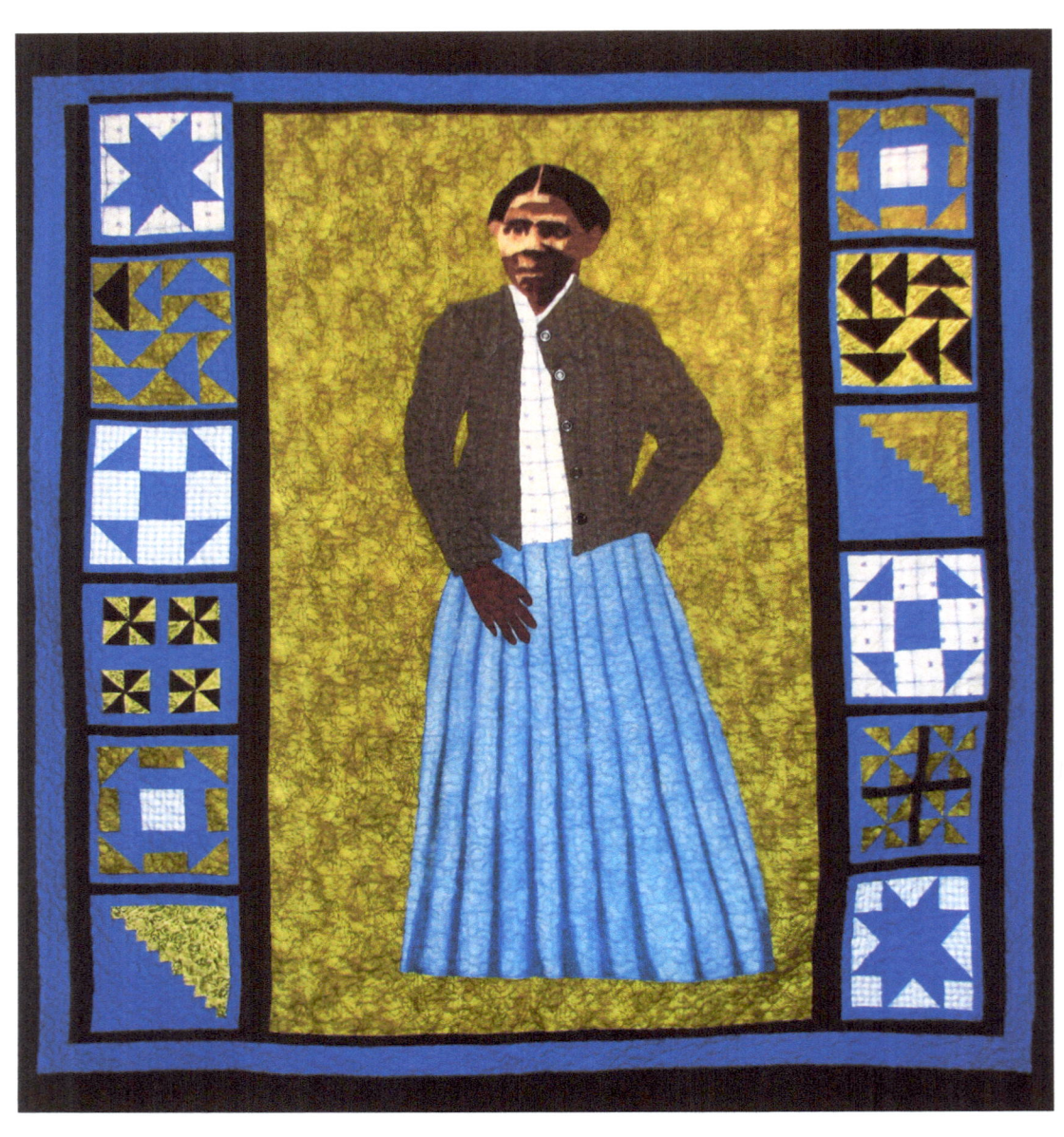

"Ms. Harriet"
Harriet Tubman
82"x94"
2008

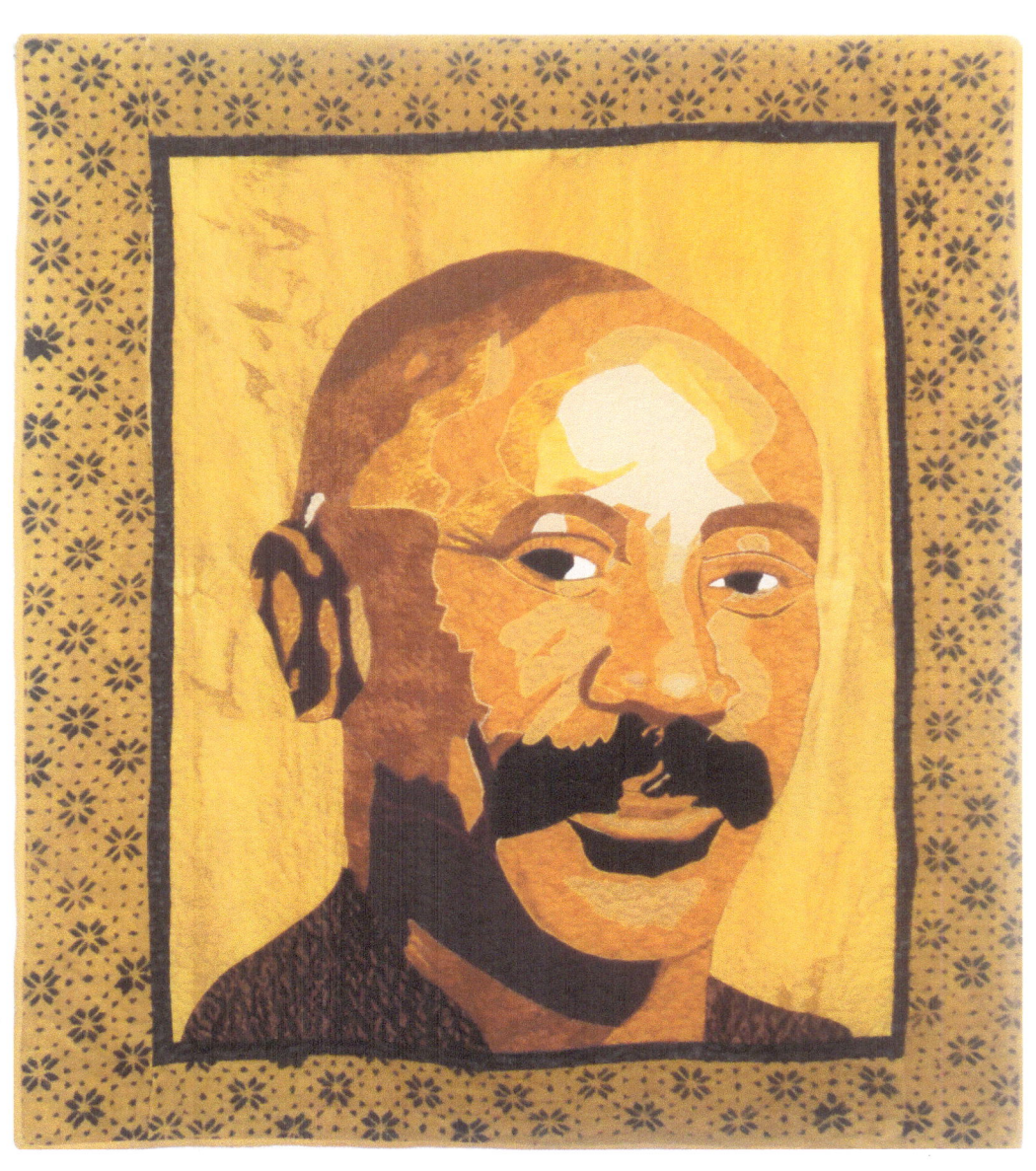

"The Fiddler"
Louis Gossett, Jr.
40"x46"
2009

About The Author

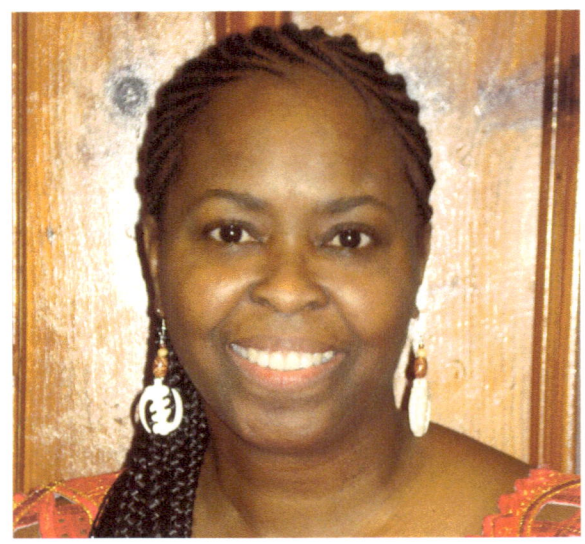

Aisha Lumumba is a fiber artist, who now lives in Atlanta, Georgia. She started exhibiting quilts in 1983. Her quilts have appeared in more than 35 exhibits throughout the United States. She has also published a 12 month wall art calendar each year for the past four years. Ms. Lumumba is available for Art Exhibits, Lectures, Quilt-Story Telling, Classes, Workshops, and Trunk Shows.

Aisha loves sewing, quilting, writing, and cooking. She is a well known vegan cook and is famous among friends for her biscuits.

Find more information about Aisha Lumumba at www.obaquilts.com

www.ingramcontent.com/pod-product-compliance
Lightning Source LLC
Chambersburg PA
CBHW050424180526
45159CB00005B/2406